Grayscale   ks

Facebook #lifeescapescoloringbooks
https://coloringbooksforadults.shop

Laura Kilgore
kilgore7098@gmail.com

This is a Life Escapes Grayscale Adult Coloring Book

Grayscale is very different than your childhood coloring books. Grayscale is preferred by those who wish to produce realistic results.

What our website has to offer:

More great adult coloring books (PDF only)
Free Color guide zip file (download)
How to color grayscale video tutorials
Download and color our freebies

Flip Through Videos
Colored pages from customers and fans
What's Inside Flip Through Videos
Coloring Greeting Cards

Our books are available in paperback on Amazon

Our website (coloringbooksforadults.shop) offers digital download PDF book files only. Print them on your paper of choice. Print the entire book or a single page at a time.

While on our website, sign up for our monthly newsletter and get a discount code for 50% off your digital orders for life.

Look at the back pages in this book for some getting started tips, instructions for downloading your free color guide and info about Life Escapes Grayscale Designers

For Business inquiries not reguarding artwork
Contact Kimberly Hawthorne at life.escapes.series@gmail.com

@Life Escapes Coloring Book for Grown-Ups   Boho Fashion By Laura Kilgore

https://adultcoloringcommunity.com/store-3/

@Life Escapes Coloring Book for Grown-Ups

Boho Fashion By Laura Kilgore

https://adultcoloringcommunity.com/store-3/

@Life Escapes Coloring Book for Grown-Ups

Boho Fashion By Laura Kilgore

https://adultcoloringcommunity.com/store-3/

@Life Escapes Coloring Book for Grown-Ups

Boho Fashion By Laura Kilgore

https://adultcoloringcommunity.com/store-3/

@Life Escapes Coloring Book for Grown-Ups

Boho Fashion By Laura Kilgore

https://adultcoloringcommunity.com/store-3/

@Life Escapes Coloring Book for Grown-Ups

Boho Fashion By Laura Kilgore

https://adultcoloringcommunity.com/store-3/

@Life Escapes Coloring Book for Grown-Ups

Boho Fashion By Laura Kilgore

https://adultcoloringcommunity.com/store-3/

@Life Escapes Coloring Book for Grown-Ups

Boho Fashion By Laura Kilgore

https://adultcoloringcommunity.com/store-3/

@Life Escapes Coloring Book for Grown-Ups

Boho Fashion By Laura Kilgore

https://adultcoloringcommunity.com/store-3/

@Life Escapes Coloring Book for Grown-Ups

Boho Fashion By Laura Kilgore

https://adultcoloringcommunity.com/store-3/

@Life Escapes Coloring Book for Grown-Ups

Boho Fashion By Laura Kilgore

https://adultcoloringcommunity.com/store-3/

@Life Escapes Coloring Book for Grown-Ups

Boho Fashion By Laura Kilgore

https://adultcoloringcommunity.com/store-3/

@Life Escapes Coloring Book for Grown-Ups

Boho Fashion By Laura Kilgore

https://adultcoloringcommunity.com/store-3/

@Life Escapes Coloring Book for Grown-Ups

Boho Fashion By Laura Kilgore

https://adultcoloringcommunity.com/store-3/

@Life Escapes Coloring Book for Grown-Ups

Boho Fashion By Laura Kilgore

https://adultcoloringcommunity.com/store-3/

@Life Escapes Coloring Book for Grown-Ups

Boho Fashion By Laura Kilgore

https://adultcoloringcommunity.com/store-3/

@Life Escapes Coloring Book for Grown-Ups

Boho Fashion By Laura Kilgore

https://adultcoloringcommunity.com/store-3/

@Life Escapes Coloring Book for Grown-Ups

Boho Fashion By Laura Kilgore

https://adultcoloringcommunity.com/store-3/

@Life Escapes Coloring Book for Grown-Ups

Boho Fashion By Laura Kilgore

https://adultcoloringcommunity.com/store-3/

@Life Escapes Coloring Book for Grown-Ups

Boho Fashion By Laura Kilgore

https://adultcoloringcommunity.com/store-3/

@Life Escapes Coloring Book for Grown-Ups

Boho Fashion By Laura Kilgore

https://adultcoloringcommunity.com/store-3/

@Life Escapes Coloring Book for Grown-Ups

Boho Fashion By Laura Kilgore

https://adultcoloringcommunity.com/store-3/

@Life Escapes Coloring Book for Grown-Ups

Boho Fashion By Laura Kilgore

https://adultcoloringcommunity.com/store-3/

@Life Escapes Coloring Book for Grown-Ups

Boho Fashion By Laura Kilgore

https://adultcoloringcommunity.com/store-3/

@Life Escapes Coloring Book for Grown-Ups

Boho Fashion By Laura Kilgore

https://adultcoloringcommunity.com/store-3/

@Life Escapes Coloring Book for Grown-Ups

Boho Fashion By Laura Kilgore

https://adultcoloringcommunity.com/store-3/

@Life Escapes Coloring Book for Grown-Ups

Boho Fashion By Laura Kilgore

https://adultcoloringcommunity.com/store-3/

@Life Escapes Coloring Book for Grown-Ups

Boho Fashion By Laura Kilgore

https://adultcoloringcommunity.com/store-3/

@Life Escapes Coloring Book for Grown-Ups

Boho Fashion By Laura Kilgore

https://adultcoloringcommunity.com/store-3/

@Life Escapes Coloring Book for Grown-Ups

Boho Fashion By Laura Kilgore

https://adultcoloringcommunity.com/store-3/

@Life Escapes Coloring Book for Grown-Ups

Boho Fashion By Laura Kilgore

https://adultcoloringcommunity.com/store-3/

@Life Escapes Coloring Book for Grown-Ups

Boho Fashion By Laura Kilgore

https://adultcoloringcommunity.com/store-3/

@Life Escapes Coloring Book for Grown-Ups

Boho Fashion By Laura Kilgore

https://adultcoloringcommunity.com/store-3/

@Life Escapes Coloring Book for Grown-Ups

Boho Fashion By Laura Kilgore

https://adultcoloringcommunity.com/store-3/

@Life Escapes Coloring Book for Grown-Ups

Boho Fashion By Laura Kilgore

https://adultcoloringcommunity.com/store-3/

@Life Escapes Coloring Book for Grown-Ups

Boho Fashion By Laura Kilgore

https://adultcoloringcommunity.com/store-3/

@Life Escapes Coloring Book for Grown-Ups

Boho Fashion By Laura Kilgore

https://adultcoloringcommunity.com/store-3/

@Life Escapes Coloring Book for Grown-Ups

Boho Fashion By Laura Kilgore

https://adultcoloringcommunity.com/store-3/

@Life Escapes Coloring Book for Grown-Ups

Boho Fashion By Laura Kilgore

https://adultcoloringcommunity.com/store-3/

@Life Escapes Coloring Book for Grown-Ups

Boho Fashion By Laura Kilgore

https://adultcoloringcommunity.com/store-3/

@Life Escapes Coloring Book for Grown-Ups

Boho Fashion By Laura Kilgore

https://adultcoloringcommunity.com/store-3/

@Life Escapes Coloring Book for Grown-Ups

Boho Fashion By Laura Kilgore

https://adultcoloringcommunity.com/store-3/

@Life Escapes Coloring Book for Grown-Ups

Boho Fashion By Laura Kilgore

https://adultcoloringcommunity.com/store-3/

@Life Escapes Coloring Book for Grown-Ups

Boho Fashion By Laura Kilgore

https://adultcoloringcommunity.com/store-3/

@Life Escapes Coloring Book for Grown-Ups

Boho Fashion By Laura Kilgore

https://adultcoloringcommunity.com/store-3/

@Life Escapes Coloring Book for Grown-Ups

Boho Fashion By Laura Kilgore

https://adultcoloringcommunity.com/store-3/

@Life Escapes Coloring Book for Grown-Ups

Boho Fashion By Laura Kilgore

https://adultcoloringcommunity.com/store-3/

@Life Escapes Coloring Book for Grown-Ups

Boho Fashion By Laura Kilgore

https://adultcoloringcommunity.com/store-3/

@Life Escapes Coloring Book for Grown-Ups

Boho Fashion By Laura Kilgore

https://adultcoloringcommunity.com/store-3/

COLOR TEST PAGE

@Life Escapes Coloring Book for Grown-Ups

Boho Fashion By Laura Kilgore

Life Escapes

https://coloringbooksforadults.shop

How to get your FREE color guide

As of April 1, 2020 we no longer honor our free pdf with amazon purchase. You may continue to download the free color guide for all our books on our website. Here is how to do it.

1. Go to https://coloringbooksforadults.shop
2. Click on top menu button that says full pdf library
3. Find the cover pic of your book and click on it
4. Scroll down to the color guide section and click the button to download the color guide

Introducing...

How to color grayscale video tutorials for sale on our website.

Watch our Basics Series Free

Go to the site address at the top then click on the "How to Color Grayscale" button in the top menu

Still Need Help?

life.escapes.series@gmail.com

https://adultcoloringcommunity.com/store-3/

Basic Grayscale Coloring Instructions

Step 1 - Choose an object in the coloring page to start with then you will need black, white and light, medium & dark shades of the color you choose. (Examples: a tree, an animal, a flower etc...)

Step 2 - With your color pencils, coloring in a circular motion, color white and light gray areas with your light color. Color dark grays with your dark color. Color medium grays with your medium color.

Tip: Overlap medium color a little ways into the light and dark areas for a seamless blend of your colors.

Step 3 - If you color with a light hand, add more layers of color to make it more visible or vibrant. Then on the highlight areas, add white over the area. Use black to outline and enhance the very darkest areas.

Tip: Keep your pencils sharp and color in a circular motion. If you have a heavy hand, move your fingers higher up on the pencil to ensure you are coloring lightly when needed.

For further techniques, methods, mediums, tips and tricks, check out our all new video tutorials on our website.

Go to https://coloringbooksforadults.shop

Then click on "How to Color Grayscale" button in the top menu

Our videos on the basics are free to watch

We want you to enjoy your coloring experience

If you are struggling with an image, please go to http://coloringbooksforadults.shop to download the color guide for this book. You will also find videos on how to color grayscale. If you still need assistance, please email Kimberly at life.escapes.series@gmail.com

Follow us on Facebook @lifeescapescoloringbooks

@Life Escapes Coloring Book for Grown-Ups   Boho Fashion By Laura Kilgore

Grayscale Adult Coloring Books

life.escapes.series@gmail.com

https://coloringbooksforadults.shop

More Great Books by Laura Kilgore

https://adultcoloringcommunity.com/store-3/

Grayscale Adult Coloring Books
life.escapes.series@gmail.com
https://coloringbooksforadults.shop

More Great Books by Kimberly Hawthorne

@Life Escapes Coloring Book for Grown-Ups

Boho Fashion By Laura Kilgore

Grayscale Adult Coloring Books

life.escapes.series@gmail.com

https://coloringbooksforadults.shop

More Great Books by Susan Mowery

Grayscale Adult Coloring Books for Men

https://adultcoloringcommunity.com/store-3/

Grayscale Adult Coloring Books
life.escapes.series@gmail.com
https://coloringbooksforadults.shop
More Great Books by Timothy Parks

@Life Escapes Coloring Book for Grown-Ups

Boho Fashion By Laura Kilgore

Grayscale Adult Coloring Books
life.escapes.series@gmail.com
https://coloringbooksforadults.shop
Life Escapes Popular Book Series'

Coming soon

Coming soon

Coming soon

Coming soon

https://adultcoloringcommunity.com/store-3/

Grayscale Adult Coloring Books
life.escapes.series@gmail.com
https://coloringbooksforadults.shop

More Life Escapes Popular Book Series'

Coming soon

End of Series

Coming soon

Coming soon

Coming soon

Coming soon

Coming soon

@Life Escapes Coloring Book for Grown-Ups

Boho Fashion By Laura Kilgore

Grayscale Adult Coloring Books
life.escapes.series@gmail.com
https://coloringbooksforadults.shop
More Life Escapes Popular Book Series'

Bloom 'n Babies	Coming soon (Bloom 'n Women)	Coming soon	Bloom 'n Critters	Bloom 'n Critters 2
Rustic Views	Rustic Views 2	Coming soon	Rustic Country Scenes	Rustic Country Scenes 2 — Coming soon
Abstract Challenge	Abstract Challenge 2	Abstract Challenge 3 — End of Series	Teddy Bear Fun	Teddy Bear Fun 2
Glorious Gowns & Dresses	Glorious Gowns & Dresses 2 — Coming soon		Christmas Fun	Christmas Fun 2 — Coming soon
Black Background Collection	Black Background Collection 2 — Coming soon		Faces of Beauty	Faces of Beauty 2 — Coming soon

https://adultcoloringcommunity.com/store-3/

NOTICE

Images used to create this coloring book have been compiled by Life Escapes grayscale designers. We do not take credit for the original artwork. We are credited for alterations and the method of our grayscaling of the original artwork.

The images used were legally compiled from sites and artists offering commercial use via free membership or paid membership. We cannot possibly know about and therefore cannot be responsible for unlawful images posted on those sites.

Some of our images sources - but not limited to...

Creative Commons
Public Domain
Expired Copyright
Free for Commercial Use
Vecteezy.com Premium Membership
Brusheezy.com Premium Membership
all-free-download.com attribution
Deviantart.com Commercial Use Ok
Dreamstime Premium Membership
Envato.com Premium Membership
freepik.com Premium Membership
Adobe Stock Photos Purchased
DepositPhotos Premium Member

freedesignfile.com
vectorfree.com
vectoropenstock.com
pxhere.com
freevector.com
pngimage.com
pngmart.com
freepngimages.com
freegreatpicture.com
pngpix.com
pixabay.com
Unsplash.com
wikimedia.commons.org
freestockphotos.biz

Disclaimer: All original artwork provided digitally is protected via a watermark of Life Escapes logo. This watermark doesn't mean we claim credit for original artwork. It is to protect the original artists which are largely unknown to us. When we know who the original artist is, we place the info below the coloring page.

With that being said, we give our customers personal use rights to our grayscaled coloring pages.

Personal use means you can make copies of uncolored images/pages in print or digital format from this book for your own personal use, but you cannot distribute them in any way without written permission from Life Escapes Adult Coloring Books owner - Kimberly Hawthorne and/or partnering artists.
This license includes but is not limited to the following:
Any and all uncolored images/pages as they appear in print, pdf, digital download and on website (http://coloringbooksforadults.shop)
Exception: free coloring pages offered on website and social media can be shared freely online when linking back to any page on coloringbooksforadults.shop.
You may NOT share coupon codes or links for digital downloads.

To report an image

For questions, comments or other...please contact us at
life.escapes.series@gmail.com

@Life Escapes Coloring Book for Grown-Ups

Boho Fashion By Laura Kilgore

Made in United States
Orlando, FL
20 June 2024